COOL CARS

This I-SPY book belongs to:_______________

Introduction

If you've ever heard someone older say "all cars look the same these days", now you can show them this great new I-Spy book! It's a pocket-sized guide to what we think are the coolest cars you'll see on the roads of Britain today – cars that really stand out and have lots of interesting features to catch your eye.
Actually, when your parents or grandparents 'do' say they can't tell one car from another, there is some truth to it. The large car-manufacturing groups compete with each other very closely, and most offer a very similar car in each segment of the car market. They are almost all computer aided design (CAD), hence their likeness. Helpfully, the European Commission has a definition for these segments. An A-segment (or A-class) car is the smallest, shortest city car like a Reva G-Wiz; a B-class is a city car, usually a hatchback, like a Ford Fiesta; a C-class car is family-sized such as a Volkswagen Golf; a D-class car is a large family saloon, usually with a separate boot, like a Vauxhall Insignia; E-class is for large executive cars like the Jaguar XF; and the F-class is for very big luxury cars, such as the Audi A8. There's also an S-class for sports cars, an M-class for multi-purpose vehicles, and a J-class for off-road vehicles. Therefore, a 'crossover' car is one that has elements of one or more class to its design.
So much for the lookalikes: what exactly is a cool car?
We've looked at most cars you're likely to see in Britain and included 120 of them that stand out from the crowd for their styling, performance, shape or distinctive features. We think these are the cars people choose to be different and admire great car design. They may not always be the best cars in their class, but they certainly have real character. Our descriptions will help you identify them, and explain their unusual aspects. You'll have to keep a careful look out, though, because they represent a fraction of the nearly 25 million cars on Britain's crowded roads. Just imagine the Michelin Man's big grin if he was driving any one of them and you'll get a good idea about why they're cool!

How to use your I-SPY book

We've included a clear picture of all our favourite cool cars you're likely to come across on a journey in Britain. Some are rare and expensive but many others are affordable and found everywhere. They're arranged in alphabetical order, so look at the pictures BEFORE you start spotting them and collecting your I-Spy points! You need 1000 points to send off for your I-Spy certificate (see page 64) but there are masses of points in every book. As you make each I-Spy, write your score in the circle.

We've included a few cool classics among the new and recent cars; if you like them best then get yourself a copy of I-Spy Classic Cars, which is crammed full of great vintage and classic machines!

ABARTH 500

There are loads of Fiat 500s on British roads, because it's proved a very popular little car for city residents. The really cool versions are the high-performance ones sold under the Abarth brand name. You'll spot them easily because they have a scorpion badge on the front. Abarths can be customised for their owners, but all Abarth 500s have wide alloy wheels, body kits and striking paint finishes, and are very fast.

I - SPY points: 20

ALFA ROMEO GIULIETTA

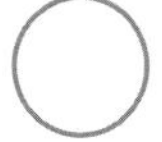

Five-door hatchbacks are sensible family cars that are often hard to tell apart. But the Giulietta's shield-shaped grille and large wheels mean it stands out. To make it look even sportier, the two rear doors are disguised by having their handles concealed in their edges, making them appear at first as a two-door. The name Giulietta was first used by Alfa Romeo in 1954, was revived in 1977 and again, for this car, in 2010.

I - SPY points: 20

ALFA ROMEO MITO

Alfa Romeo has been making sporty cars since before World War I, but until the MiTo came along in 2008, it had never offered a very small super-mini-type car. Big headlights and gri give a bold appearance while the narrow side windows make it clear this is a tight fit for four people! The name MiTo mixes the Italian cities of 'Milan', whe the car was designed, and 'Torino' (Turin), where it is made

 **I - SPY points: 10**

ALFA ROMEO SPIDER

This two-seater sports car with its thrust-forward, pointed nose is quite a rare sight even in its home country of Italy, as less than 13,000 examples were made. Alfa Romeo stopped selling it in 2010. It's very unusual for a sports car in that is was offered with a turbodiesel engine, but like all real roadsters it has a folding canvas roof for top-down fun motoring.

 **I - SPY points: 30**

ASTON MARTIN DB7

Low and wide with its headlights under sloping covers, the DB7 looks expensive and fast – which it was, with its supercharged straight-six cylinder engine. With only about 7,000 of them built between 1994 and 2004, it will be an unusual 'spy' for you, and you could see it either as a sleek coupe or a smart convertible known as the DB7 Volante.

I - SPY points: 35

ASTON MARTIN RAPIDE

his is the four-door saloon
nember of the Aston Martin
amily. You'll need to be sharp-
yed to tell because it's styled to
ook like a two-door. It will roar
p to a 188mph top speed,
owered by the 6-litre V12
ngine mounted upfront, and it
osts about £140,000. Look out
or the twin louvres on the bonnet
op, to keep that huge engine
entilated.

I - SPY points: 40

ASTON MARTIN V8 VANTAGE

In 2005, Britain's Aston Martin decided to compete head-on against Germany's Porsche 911 with its own compact supercar. But while the Porsche has its engine at the back, the Vantage has its V8 at the front. The body of the car appears to wrap itself tightly around the engine, wheels and two passengers, with a short rear end. The front grille has the traditional 'clipped rectangle' Aston Martin shape.

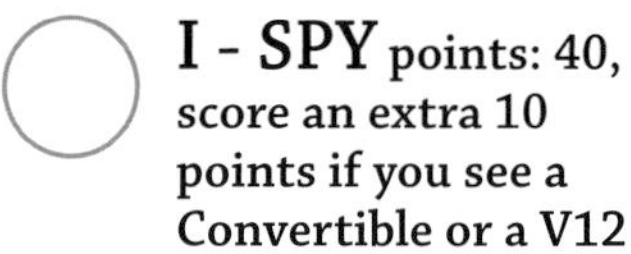

I - SPY points: 40, score an extra 10 points if you see a Convertible or a V12 Vantage version.

AUDI A2

This little car, made between 1999 and 2005, looks a bit weird with its small wheels and stubby bonnet, but it's a clever design. This was the first family car with an entirely aluminium body and frame; aluminium weighs less than steel, and this helps the light A2 use the minimum of fuel. There's no opening bonnet; water and oil are poured in through nozzles hidden behind the front panel.

I - SPY points: 15

UDI A5 CABRIOLET

his broad and handsome
onvertible may only have two
loors but inside there's plenty of
oom for four people to spread
ut and relax. It's a great car
or family open-top cruising
n sunny days, but there is an
lectronically-operated roof
n case you start to feel a few
aindrops! If you see the word
quattro' on the back then you'll
now it's a four-wheel drive
ersion.

I - SPY points: 20, score an extra 5 points if you see the similar looking but higher-performance S5 Cabriolet.

UDI Q7

ou'll certainly notice the Q7
ecause it's one of the biggest
assenger cars on the road.
here's an 'edge' running right
ound the car through its front
poiler, wheelarches and side
kirts. All Q7s have four-wheel
lrive and most have either a
-litre turbodiesel or 4.2-litre
etrol engine. But a very few
ome with a mighty V12
urbodiesel engine, this model
osting over £100,000.

I - SPY points: 20

AUDI R8

This two-seater sports car is mid-engined, and you can see the air intakes for its V8 or V10 power unit just behind the doors – they're emphasised with a panel painted black in contrast to the rest of the body. Through the glass rear window the engine is on display, and some R8s have engine bay lighting to show it off at night! Top speed is 197mph for the V10.

AUDI TT

The smooth lines, with no obvious bumpers, of the original Audi TT of 1998 were inspired by German Bauhaus architecture and speed record cars of the 1950s. You'd never guess that, underneath, the chassis shares much with the Volkswagen Golf. The second-generation TT arrived in 2006 – it's longer and wider, and with a diesel option. TTs come as 2+2 coupes or two-seater roadsters; score for any you see.

BENTLEY CONTINENTAL GT

First introduced in 2003, this beautiful-looking four-seater GT car has many stand-out details, like its four separate headlights, its mesh grille (designed to collapse if it hits a pedestrian), and the old-fashioned bodywork lines that suggest the separate wings of classic Bentleys. Under the long bonnet is a twin-supercharged W12 engine. Unusually, this car holds the world speed record for driving on ice, at 205mph!

I - SPY points: 35

BENTLEY MULSANNE

Named after the long straight at Le Mans, this luxury limousine can be customised for each, very rich owner, but even in standard form each car takes 15 weeks to build by craftsmen and women at Bentley's Cheshire factory. The stainless steel exterior trim alone takes 10 hours to handfinish. The engine is a 6.75-litre V8. Look for the large mesh grille, big round headlights, and sculpted front wings. Plus, it's over 5.5m long!

I - SPY points: 45

BMW M6

This is one of the fastest and most expensive cars that BMW makes. It can reach 60mph from standstill in just 4.1sec thanks to the 500bhp of power from its V10 engine, and the top speed is artificially limited to 155mph. Clever aerodynamics mean it doesn't need a huge rear spoiler, but the roof is carbonfibre, the boot and wings plastic, and the bonnet and doors aluminium to reduce weight.

I - SPY points: 35, score an extra 5 points if you see the convertible version.

BMW X6

This is a unique-looking car – one that is known as a 'crossover' in the car world. That's because it mixes one type of car with another, in this case the lower part of a four-wheel drive vehicle with the upper part of a fastback luxury saloon. It stands very tall on the road and features hugely flared-out wheelarches. It has a big V8 engine.

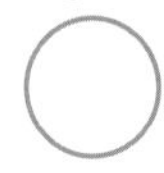

I - SPY points: 25

BMW Z4

It takes only 20 seconds to raise or lower the concealed metal hardtop of the current Z4, a two-seater sports car. Like all BMWs, it has a grille that some people liken to a pair of kidneys, and in the Z4's case they are flatter and wider than almost any BMW before it. Look out for the BMW badges on front, back and sides.

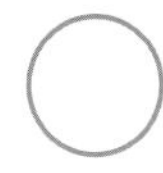

I - SPY points: 20

BUGATTI VEYRON

This truly amazing machine is the fastest road-legal production car in the world. In its current Supersport version with 1200bhp of engine power, it can hit 267mph. It has a horseshoe-shaped front grille dropping almost to ground level and a curved and bulky rear end in which the 8-litre W16 engine, (16 cylinder) lives. Very few are made each year, so seeing one will be quite an event.

I - SPY points: 50

CATERHAM SEVEN

This two-seater sports car has often been described as a 'four-wheeled motorbike' because of its exciting driving responses, and also because it's stripped down to the very basics. It has separate mudguards for each wheel, standalone headlights, no boot, a tiny windscreen and a snug cockpit with a tight hood. Beware of look-alikes: only a Caterham will have a big '7' across its front grille.

I - SPY points: 30

CHEVROLET VOLT

The Volt stands out, with its deep side windows, thrust-forward look and rear lights that wrap around the bodysides. The really interesting bit is inside, though. This is a petrol-electric hybrid. The car's electric engine has a range of 40 miles (it can be plugged in at a mains socket to recharge) but when its battery power is used up it can be switched to a 1.4-litre petrol engine to extend its range.

CHRYSLER 300C TOURING

There aren't many cool estate cars, but this American-designed Chrysler has real character to it. The chrome front grille and the huge wheels look impressive, and the low roofline and narrow windows produce a sporty, squat appearance ...even if they make it less roomy inside than some rivals. You can score for any 300C you see including the saloon and the new-generation model.

I - SPY points: 20

CHRYSLER CROSSFIRE

An interesting compact coupe only made for four years between 2003 and 2007, so you won't see many of them. It's a bold design, with a wide front grille, polished metal windscreen surround, a short back end and cross-hatched side air intakes from which it derives its name. There's a convertible model too that has a fabric folding roof instead of the coupe version with a glass rear window.

I - SPY points: 30

CHRYSLER DELTA

Chrysler is an American make of car but its smaller models sold in Europe are actually built in Italy, where this car is sold as the Lancia Delta. It's an athletic looking five-door hatchback with a high side window line, a deep hatchback screen, thin rear light clusters and a long frontage. The upper section of these cars is finished in black and look distinctive.

I - SPY points: 25, score 5 extra points if you see a Lancia Delta version, when you're on holiday in mainland Europe.

CHRYSLER PT CRUISER

On sale from 2000 to 2010, this unusual family car drew its inspiration from 1930s cars driven by Hollywood movie gangsters or customised cars of hot rod enthusiasts. That's why it appears to have separate mudguards over each wheel and an old-fashioned slatted chrome grille. Apart from its looks, it was entirely modern. Over 1.3 million were sold, some of which were the rare two-door convertible model with built-in roll-over bar.

I - SPY points: 15, double for a convertible

I - SPY points: 25

CITROËN 2CV

Millions of these curvy economy cars were made in France until the late 1980s, and quite a few are still cherished by their owners. The car was nicknamed the 'tin snail' for its rounded look, and you can easily see why. The wheels are housed under separate mudguards, with the rear ones closed in and the headlights standing proud on top of the front ones. All 2CVs have a fabric top that can be fully rolled back to enjoy the sun.

I - SPY points: 25

CITROËN C3 PLURIEL

The cute Pluriel is about as close to a '*Transformer*' toy as any production car has got. You can roll back the full-length 'cabriolet' sunroof for as much sunlight and fresh air as you want or, with the curved roof bars removed, have the car as a full four-seater convertible. And as if that wasn't enough, fold down the rear seats and it becomes a useful pick-up.

CITROËN C-CROSSER

This stylish 'sport crossover' car has high ground clearance and upright seating, so you won't be surprised to know that it has four wheel drive and can perform as well off road as on it. You might see very similar cars carrying the Peugeot 4007 or Mitsubishi Outlander names; they're all built in the same factory, but only Citroën has this distinctive frontal design.

I - SPY points: 15, score only 10 points if you see the Peugeot or Mitsubishi editions.

CITROËN DS3

When you see a small family three-door hatchback with a striking two-tone paint scheme then it will probably be a DS3. Customers can choose from many colour combinations. The car also has unusual triangular central roof pillars and LCD bar running lights in slanted slots on its two front corners. Look out too for the DS3's unique badge on front and back.

I - SPY points: 10

:ITROËN NEMO ЛULTISPACE

 you feel like 'finding Nemo' ıen keep an eye out for this dd-looking – but very practical compact 'people-carrier' 'om Citroën. It was launched ı 2008. It has twin van-like loors at the back and sliding ɜar passenger doors. The iangulated side windows, ulging front bumper and huge ircular emblem at the back are ery distinctive. Fiat's edition is alled the Qubo.

I - SPY points: 10, score 15 points for the Fiat Qubo.

DAIHATSU COPEN

You can't buy any Daihatsus in the UK now because imports to Europe from Japan stopped in 2011. The 1.3-litre Copen was always rare anyway. It's a tiny two-seater sports convertible that looks a bit like an early Audi TT that got shrunk in a carwash! Despite its very small dimensions, the Copen still has a metal roof that folds away electronically at the touch of a button.

I - SPY points: 30

FERRARI 458 ITALIA

This two-seater 202mph supercar is the very latest mid-engined Ferrari – the 4.5-litre V8 engine is positioned right behind the driver and passenger. The body design appears to fold one layer over another, and the car has five-spoke light alloy wheels through which the powerful brakes can be seen. Its 'active' aerodynamic design produces cooling air for the engine, entering ducts beneath the car.

I - SPY points: 45

FERRARI F430

Introduced in 2004, the F430 has been replaced by the 458 Italia, but you may see one from time to time – they were popular with Premier League footballers and pop stars. There are upper and lower air intakes on the side behind the doors, and the mid-mounted V8 engine is visible under a glass rear cover. There was a convertible F430 Spider too; both can reach over 190mph.

I - SPY points: 40

I - SPY points: 50

FERRARI FF

The FF is something really different from Ferrari. Like other cars from this famous Italian company, it has a massively powerful V12 engine, this time mounted in the front, and can break the 200mph speed barrier. However, it is a hatchback with four seats just like a normal car. It's also the first four-wheel drive Ferrari. At £227,000 it's very expensive but if you see one you'll instantly recognise its 'estate car' profile.

IAT MULTIPLA

ıe Multipla was dropped from e Fiat range in 2010 after ɜing on sale for 12 years. It's compact family people-carrier ıd is very unusual in that it seats ҡ people with three in front and ·ee in the back. That's why it's little wider than competitors. ırly cars had additional driving ıhts positioned just below the indscreen and headlights sunk ·o the chubby nose; later ones ıve a more conventional front.

I - SPY points: 10

FORD KUGA

Although it has a high-riding stance and generous ground clearance, Ford's big-selling Kug comes in both two and four wheel drive versions. It has twin raised 'blades' on top of the bonnet and rails on either side c the roof for carrying a roof load Meanwhile, at the front, it has a double 'snout' with upper and lower air intakes.

I - SPY points: 10

FORD MUSTANG

There have been loads of different Mustang types since the first took the car world by storm in 1964. The current one looks a lot like 1960s Mustangs, with headlights and grille under the bonnet's 'brow' and the original car's body side moulding lines. There are fastback, coupe and convertible versions. Ford makes the Mustang in left-hand drive form only, so there aren't many on UK roads.

I - SPY points: 40

FORD PUMA

Although this perky little coupe was last sold in the UK in 2002, there are still about 40,000 of them on our roads. It has a bonnet that slopes down at the front and a high tail concealing a hatchback third door. The design of the car is very sculptural, with wheels appearing to bulge out of its sides, and headlights glazed in below clear plastic covers. You'd never guess it was closely related to the humble Ford Fiesta...

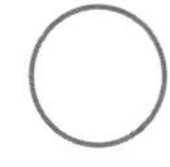

I - SPY points: 15

FORD STREETKA

From the front this tiny two-seater convertible closely resembles the very common Ford Ka MkI which you can still see all over Britain, but at the back it has a boot lid and not a hatchback and a neat exhaust pipe that exits in the middle of the car through a hole in the bumper. The roof is a simple fabric folding hood. And in case you were wondering, you pronounce it 'street car'.

I - SPY points: 30

HONDA CIVIC TYPE-R

The Type R is the high-performance model in the last generation Civic range (the whole Civic series having been fully updated – there won't be a replacement Type R for a few years). The old Civic was alread a dramatic looking car, with a short bonnet and aggressive lines. The Type R adds a deep front spoiler and a rear air dam; there's a clear plastic strip across the whole front of the car, with headlights behind it. It has a responsive and fast 201bhp 2-litre engine.

 **I - SPY points: 20**

HONDA CR-Z

This very small coupe is unmissable on the road, thanks to its dramatic styling – viewed from the side, the swooping panels seem to present a big metal 'Z' in shape. It has a large snout with the number plate right in the middle of the grille. The CR-Z is a petrol-electric hybrid, so offers very good fuel economy, but can still sprint to 60mph in 10sec.

 **I - SPY points: 25**

I - SPY points: 15

HONDA FR-V

The chunky-looking FR-V is a great car for a busy family, especially where one of the parents is running a small business. This is because, with the flick of three levers, it can quickly be converted from a people-carrier to a small van. You'll notice that the sides of the car are flat and upright; this is because it has three seats upfront, as well as in the back.

HONDA S2000

Here is a traditional two-seater sports car from Honda, with engine at the front and drive to the rear wheels. It's a dart-shaped roadster where the bonnet is barely higher than the tops of the front wheels, and the headlamps look like narrowed eyes! If you see one with the hood down then you'll notice the twin steel hoops behind the front seats, which protect the driver and passenger if the car rolls over.

I - SPY points: 20

HUMMER H3

This 4x4 off-roader is big, boxy and looks super-tough. It has square wheelarches to accommodate its huge wheels, and a massive, chrome-effect grille at the front with the word H-U-M-M-E-R spelt out across the top. There is a step below the doors to help you climb up into its cabin. Made only between 2005 and 2008, there are a handful in the UK, where it was sold with right-hand drive.

 **I - SPY points: 30**

HYUNDAI COUPE

When this four-seater was sold in the UK between 2003 and 2008, it was the coolest car yet from South Korean manufacturer Hyundai. Some people thought it even seemed like a small version of the Ferrari 456GT – the styling lines along the sides look a bit similar. It has big headlight openings but a tiny front air intake, and some models have a neat air dam at the back.

 **I - SPY points: 10**

HYUNDAI VELOSTER

Designers at Hyundai's 'Premium Youth Lab' studios really have made the 'face' of the Veloster like nothing else on the road, but it's even more unusual at the sides. On the driver's side is one large single door, but on the passenger side there's a front *and* a rear door, Check out the wild dashboard and touch-screen design too. The engine is a four-cylinder 1.6, with or without turbocharger.

I - SPY points: 30

AGUAR E-TYPE

you love older cars then you eed to get *I-Spy Classic Cars*, vhich is packed with historic nodels. But we've included the -type here too because there's othing else quite like it…and 's been cool since the day it vas launched in 1961. Long, leek and glamorous, it's also vind-cheating – in fact, it was lesigned like an upside-down ircraft wing to help it stick to ne road!

I - SPY points: 25

JAGUAR XF

This good-looking luxury saloon is the British alternative to rivals like BMW, Lexus and Mercedes-Benz. It has a unique style, especially at the front, where a growling 'big cat' face sits in the centre of a mesh grille, with slanted headlights on either side, and at the back, where a Jaguar emblem 'leaps' above a strip between the rear light clusters. Engines range from thrifty four-cylinder diesel to powerful 5-litre V8 petrol.

I - SPY points: 10

JAGUAR XJ

You'll often see this big, impressive Jaguar model on TV, as the Prime Minister uses one for visits around the country. It has a large simple front grille, a high waistline, a very large high boot and rear light clusters rising up along the tops of the rear wings. The passenger compartment is kitted out like a top-class hotel, and even with a 3-litre diesel engine, performance is impressive – 155mph top speed, 0-60mph in 6.4sec.

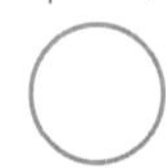

I - SPY points: 15

JAGUAR XJ-S

Here is another Jaguar which, like the E-type, looks like nothing else. It's a low, wide car with large looking wheels. The front grille is a thin strip, with separate oval headlight pods (the lights are either oval or twin sets of round ones). On the more common coupe, the boot lid is flat but the rear wings rise up to meet the roof, resembling the 'flying buttresses' that support an ancient cathedral wall.

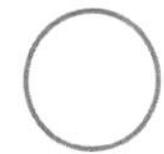

I - SPY points: 20

AGUAR XK

\ bit like its E-type ancestor of
;0 years ago, the sporty XK has
lefinite 'hips' – the line of its
vings rises over the rear wheels.
his attractive luxury GT car has
n oval grille and, in the case
f the super-fast XKR-S version,
as extra ventilation slots in front
f the bonnet and front wings.
his is a four-seater – just – but
ne seats in the back can only
ccommodate very small
hildren. There are both coupe
nd convertible versions.

I - SPY points: 20

JEEP WRANGLER

When most people think of a Jeep, it's the Wrangler type that comes to mind, with its separate mudguards front and back, round headlights either side of a row of vertical air intakes, and the familiar 'Jeep' name sitting above it. Big fat wheels hint at its four-wheel drive abilities on rough terrain. You might see a Wrangler as a two- or four-door, hardtop or convertible, but they all share a strong family resemblance inspired by military vehicles of the past.

I - SPY points: 15

JEEP COMMANDER

This is a very large, seven-seater SUV, standing for 'sport-utility vehicle', with a boxy, slab-like, squared-off image. You'll notice a slight 'step' in its roofline, which allows the second and third rows of seats to be higher-mounted than the front one, so everyone has good visibility. Some Commanders even have three sunroofs! You can probably guess just by looking at it that it's four-wheel drive, and has powerful V6 diesel or V8 petrol engines.

I - SPY points: 20

KIA CEE'D

Some may think that the Cee'd isn't particularly exciting, but it certainly got the approval of the team on BBC2's car show *Top Gear*. Not on its *'Cool Wall'*, admittedly, but featured in the *'Star in a Reasonably-Priced Car'* spot introduced by Jeremy Clarkson. It follows in the wheel tracks of the Suzuki Liana and Chevrolet Lacetti. The Cee'd is a neat-looking car, about the size of a Ford Focus or Volkswagen Golf, and is made in Slovakia.

I - SPY points: 10

KIA SOUL

This is a small car for someone who might have chosen a Ford Fiesta or Volkswagen Polo but wanted something a bit different. It's shaped like a small van, with a vertical rear end and light clusters mounted high up on its rear corners. It has bulging wheelarches and, at the front, what Kia calls its 'tiger nose' front grille. The Soul was designed in California.

I - SPY points: 10

LAMBORGHINI AVENTADOR

This incredible supercar, which costs a quarter of a million pounds and can reach 217mph, looks like a thin wedge, narrowly angled against the road surface. Gigantic scoops on each side of its carbonfibre body feed air to the 6.5-litre V12 engine in the middle of the car, while flattened hexagonal scoops at the front ventilate brakes and cool the cockpit. Sprinting to 60mph from standstill takes just 2.8sec.

I - SPY points: 50

LAMBORGHINI GALLARDO

The 'baby' Lamborghini packs a mighty performance punch from its 5.0- or 5.2-litre V10 engine, which is mid-mounted. It's a wedge-shaped car, with its headlights and bonnet forming a continuous line with the large, flat windscreen. Engine air intakes are behind the doors. You might see a Gallardo as either a coupe or a convertible roadster and, like all Lamborghinis, they have a charging bull on their logos.

I - SPY points: 45

LAND ROVER DEFENDER

The rugged, four-wheel drive Defender is found in a wide variety of different forms. It's built on a separate chassis frame and can be adapted for all sorts of tasks, as well as being sold in short-, long- and extra-long wheelbase versions as estate, van or pick-up. They all share the same, boxy look with round headlights and square, open wheelarches allowing the wheels plenty of clearance when off-road.

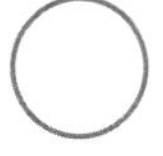 **I - SPY points: 5**

OTUS ELISE

otus's neat little sports car is ke a Ferrari or Lamborghini in iniature, with side air intakes cool the mid-mounted engine which is a 1.6 or 1.8-litre urcylinder unit made by Toyota and thin, flat headlight units ing on top of the short bonnet. ke the bigger mid-engined ports cars, the Elise is very low the ground. With the roof in lace, the side windows are xtremely narrow; once it's emoved, it's wind-in-your-hair me!

I - SPY points: 20

LOTUS ESPRIT

This Lotus was on sale between 1976 and 2004 in various forms, and has starred in several movies, including the James Bond film *The Spy Who Loved Me* in 1977, in which an Esprit becomes a submarine. The car you'll most likely see on the road is the MkII shown here. It has a long, shark-like, overhung front section with concealed headlights that pop up when switched on. The engine air intakes are behind the side windows, and there are several different types of rear spoiler.

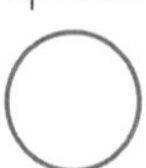

I - SPY points: 25

LOTUS EVORA

Like many great racing and spor cars, the Evora is mid-engined – and has fantastic roadholding because it's well balanced – but there are two seats in the back for small children. The twin blacl grilles on the bonnet take air intc the cockpit, while at the back it has a spoiler designed in, rather than bolted on, to help the airflow press the car down on to the road.

I - SPY points: 30

MASERATI GRANTURISMO

A long, low and curvaceous four-seater GT car from Italy, its name says it all; *gran turismo* is Italian for 'grand touring', which is exactly what this machine is designed for – fast trips over long distances, travelling in great luxury. The lines of the car curve in and out from front to back, with a prominent, low-down 'snout' at the front and hugely flared openings for the alloy wheels. The V8 engine makes an exciting growling noise!

I - SPY points: 30

MASERATI QUATTROPORTE

This Italian-made sports saloon is big and handsome on the outside, and you can easily tell it's a Maserati from the chrome 'trident' emblems on its radiator grille and on the roof pillars behind the side windows. Have a look inside if you get the chance – the cabin of the Quattroporte (the word means 'four-door' in Italian) is beautifully trimmed in leather – and try to hear the exciting bark from its V8 engine.

I - SPY points: 30

I - SPY points: 50, score an extra 10 points of you see one of the truly massive Maybach 62 limousines.

MAYBACH 57

Royalty and celebrities around th world, from Madonna and Simo Cowell to Formula 1 boss Bernie Ecclestone, own Maybachs. It's a German-made rival to limousines from Bentley and Rolls Royce, although with its smaller front grille and fairly plain styling it doesn't stand out like the British duo, and actually looks like a giant-size Mercedes-Benz. Cool options include a voice-activated rear sunroof.

I - SPY points: 15

MAZDA CX-5 SPORT

This is a very spacious and practical small sport-utility vehicle (SUV) with a four-wheel drive option. With either a 2.0-litre petrol or 2.2-litre diesel engine, it's good to drive, and has excellent handling and roadholding. It's also an interesting car to look at, with a high bonnet and lots of swoopy lines playing around the blackplastic-edged wheelarches and its big wheels; check out the way daylight is reflected by the scalloped sides.

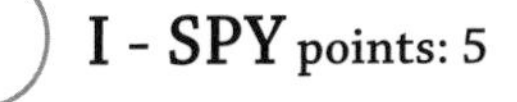

MAZDA MX-5

This MX-5 is the latest version of Mazda's rear wheeled drive two-seater – the third generation of the world's best-selling sports car. It is available with either a traditional fabric roof, that has to be folded by hand, or an electrically operated folding metal hardtop. Headlights are small and thin and there is a bulge right in the middle of the bonnet top. Score for any MX-5 that you see.

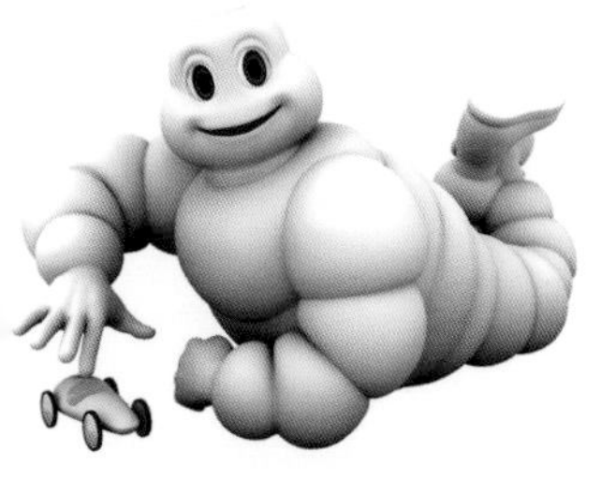

I - SPY points: 15

MAZDA RX-8

There's some hidden magic to this four-seater GT car; when the front doors are opened, two small rear doors are revealed and can be opened too, making access to the back seats really easy. Production stopped in 2012, which makes it (for now) the last production car with a rotary engine; it has twin revolving rotors, rather than pistons pumping up and down, providing smooth delivery of power...but heavy fuel consumption.

MCLAREN MP4-12C

McLaren is a name very familiar from the Formula 1 racing circuit but, until recently, it has rarely been seen on the road. McLaren decided to take on Ferrari road cars with this stunning mid-engined coupe. Although the styling, compared to some supercars, is quite plain and simple, it has amazing doors – they open up and outwards, like a bat's wings.

I - SPY points: 50

MERCEDES-BENZ A-CLASS

Many of the new A-Class you see will have a full-length glass sunroof and big alloy wheels. But they will all have the distinctive styling of the smallest 'Merc', with a sweeping, wave-like shape moulded into the sides. Although this five-door hatchback doesn't look too different from rivals from the back, the huge star logo on the front proves it could only be a Mercedes-Benz, even if it is the smallest one you can buy.

I - SPY points: 15

MERCEDES-BENZ CLS SHOOTING BRAKE

This is probably the coolest and most unusual estate car on the road today. Its graceful and flowing lines, such as the gentle, tapering curve made by the side window shape, are miles away from the usual 'two-box' profile estate cars possess. It's still very roomy inside for both people and luggage. With the AMG-tuned 5.6-litre V8 engine behind that broad horizontal grille, it's an extremely rapid car.

I - SPY points: 20, score an extra 10 points for the AMG version

IERCEDES-BENZ -CLASS

his off-road vehicle looks like was designed using a ruler! hen again, it was first seen in he 1970s as a high-quality vorkhorse for extreme terrain ke mud, snow and rocks, in the lays when most people drove a 4x4 vehicle on the road only to ow a horsebox. The indicators re in little pods on top of the ont wings. The most expensive ersion with a V8 engine costs lmost £125,000, so it is less kely to be used by farmers hese days.

I - SPY points: 20

MERCEDES-BENZ SLK

The original SLK of 1996 was the world's first modern sports car with a built-in folding metal hardtop. Three generations on and that is still a strong feature of this neat two-seater, which is easily spotted from the front due to its shiny metal bar across the grille with the Mercedes star huge as its centrepiece. It has roll-over hoops behind each seat. Engines choice ranges from an eager 1.8-litre to a hugely powerful AMG-modified 5.5-litre V8, along with diesel versions.

MERCEDES-BENZ SLS AMG

This car is at the very top of the Mercedes sporting range, and at almost £180,000, with 571bhp of power from a 6.2-litre AMG engine, and a top speed of 197mph, it really is quite a car. The Roadster is a great looking car but the coupe shown here, with its gullwing doors that rise open from a central spot in the car's roof, looks sensational.

MGB

I - SPY points: 20

Originally on sale between 1962 and 1981, there are still a surprisingly large number of these sports cars, in open roadster and fastback GT form, on Britain's roads. This is because you can still get all the parts to keep them going and there is a large owner's club, but also because owners love driving them. They are old-fashioned cars, with no electronic gadgets or modern safety features, but they're fun to drive and very simple to maintain.

MGF/TF

When the MG name was revived in 1995 it was with this cute mid-engined two-seater sports car. The line of the body rises gently from front to rear, and the cockpit is a snug fit for two people only. The car was thoroughly modified to become the TF in 2002, which gave it a new all-round bodykit, a re-designed front, and reshaped air intakes just behind the doors. Score for either an F or a TF.

MINI 'CLASSIC'

The original Mini is only 3 metres long and is an extremely compact car for four people. It remains an amazing little car, with handling like a go-kart and a cheeky character with its tiny bonnet, round headlights, chubby body shape and rain gutters running around the edge of the roof. Over 5 million were built between 1959 and 2001, making it the best-selling British car ever.

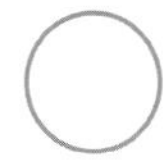 **I - SPY points: 10**

MINI CONVERTIBLE

The all-new Mini was introduced in 2001, as a completely new car but with all the charm of the original. Everyone seems to love it, but we're not giving any points for the saloon version that you see everywhere: you only score if you see one of the convertible models. With the hood raised, you have to look hard to tell it apart, but with the electric roof lowered you'll always see the roll-over hoops behind the rear seats.

 **I - SPY points: 5**

MINI COUPE

This probably won't be the Mini your mum or dad chooses because it is strictly a two-seater fun car aimed at people who don't need to worry about carrying much in the back!. The windscreen is angled 13 degrees lower than on other Minis, and the 'helmet' roof is made from aluminium. It's very cosy inside. At the back is a spoiler that automatically rises at speeds above 50mph.

I - SPY points: 25

MITSUBISHI I-MIEV

This is a pure electric car, and you might see lookalikes called the Citroën C-Zero or Peugeot iOn – all three are actually built by Mitsubishi. The tall, narrow car has almost no bonnet at all and deep side windows, with its headlights mounted high up just below the windscreen, and from many angles it looks quite like a four-door version of a Smart car. With a fairly limited range, most will be driven in towns and cities.

I - SPY points: 35

MORGAN AERO SUPERSPORTS

An unusual British sports car that mixes high technology with tradition. It has flowing separate mudguards with its big headlights smoothed into the front either side of a 'waterfall' grille. The roof has detachable aluminium panels that can be stored in the boot, which comes to a V-shaped point at the back. The cockpit is narrow and snug, and the handmade car is powered by a BMW V8 engine.

MORGAN PLUS 4

Morgan celebrated its 100th anniversary in 2010; it's the oldest car manufacturer still owned by the founder's family. It's been making cars like this one since 1954...and even then it wasn't a very modern-looking roadster. The hand-built cars still have a separate chassis, with body frame made of seasoned ash timber, although the engine is the very latest Ford V6 or four-cylinder. Owners enjoy 'vintage' motoring with modern reliability.

MORGAN THREE-WHEELER

Morgan amazed the car world by returning to three-wheelers in 2011 after a gap of 59 years; it was immediately overwhelmed with orders for the car, which has its single wheel at the back. Its twin-cylinder engine, which comes from a Harley-Davidson motorbike, is completely exposed at the front, while the body, with its open cockpit, tapers to a point at the back. It is huge fun to drive, and has lightning acceleration.

I - SPY points: 50

NISSAN 370Z

Unlike most other Nissans you can buy in the UK, the 370Z has drive going to the rear wheels only. Combined with the 326bhp of power from its 3.7-litre V6 engine at the front, this makes for a true sports car driving experience. The 370Z has the much-loved long bonnet/short rear end look, with the bodywork bulging dramatically around the wheels, and a seemingly tiny cabin with a low roofline.

I - SPY points: 25

NISSAN FIGARO

Although this car looks like it has driven straight out of the 1950s, with its chrome details, painted wheel discs and roll-back convertible roof, it was built in 1991 as a limited edition of 20,000. They are usually two-tone, with a white roof above a pastel-coloured body. It's very easy and economical to drive because, under those retro clothes, the Figaro is identical to an automatic Nissan Micra, and owners love them.

I - SPY points: 30

NISSAN GT-R

The GT-R seems to have bodywork rippling with muscles, and indeed this big two-door, four-seater coupe provides a formidable performance from its 3.8-litre V6 engine, tuned like a racing cars to give 550bhp. In fact, the whole car has been developed from competition cars, and the GT-R will reach a 193mph top speed. The chunky front end appears to leap forward, while at the back a tail spoiler on the huge boot sits above four circular rear lights.

I - SPY points: 35

NISSAN JUKE

One of the most unusual-looking
amily hatchbacks on sale and,
what's more, the Juke was
designed and built in Britain. It's
a cross between an off-roader
and a coupe. Not the roomiest
car inside but still cool and with
a great-looking dashboard. The
Juke has huge bulges around
each wheel, while at the front
he indicators are on top of
he bonnet and the headlights
are under the corners of a big
grinning' air intake.

I - SPY points: 10

NISSAN LEAF

he Leaf isn't an electric version
of a Nissan model; it's a
pecially-designed five-door
hatchback that *only* comes as a
pure electric car. So, there's no
adiator grille at the front, but
here is an opening panel, with
he Nissan logo in the middle of
, hiding the recharging point for
he lithium ion batteries. Check
out the swoopy lines and light
clusters front and back.

NISSAN QASHQAI

The Qashqai is an incredibly popular family car in Britain because it's comfortable, stylish and useful, with four-wheel drive an option for a car that already has upright seating and high ground clearance. The window line slopes upwards towards the back, while a black-lower body section helps to make this car look like it rides high over all sorts of terrain; the Qashqai+2 is a slightly longer version, with two extra seats right at the back. Most Qashqais seen in the UK are made in Nissan's Sunderland factory.

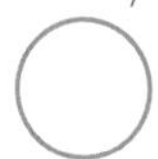
I - SPY points: 5

PEUGEOT 207 CC

The open version of the big-selling 207 comes with an ingenious folding metal hardtop that makes it a true coupe-convertible – hence the CC name. The windscreen is steeply raked right over the two front seats, enabling the short roof section to connect up with it. Peugeot's lion badge is framed in a large four-sided section on the nose of the car and strips along the sides stop the doors getting damaged in tight parking spots.

I - SPY points: 25

PEUGEOT 3008 HYBRID4

This chunky-looking crossover vehicle has lots of Peugeot's familiar design touches, like the hefty front-end with its cheese grater grille. The arrow-shaped rear light clusters merge with the 'hips' of the wing line. Inside is a technical world first – a diesel/electric hybrid power system. Batteries power the rear wheels, and a 2-litre diesel engine powers the front ones. Electric power is used for short trips making it environmentally friendly. At an average 75mpg, it's extremely frugal with fuel.

I - SPY points: 15

'EUGEOT RCZ

his aggressive, low-to-the-ground oupe is the sportiest Peugeot ·ver, making it a rival to cars ke the Audi TT. The low body hape is full of big curves, with ıe rear portion of the car looking uite self-contained. Two bright ıetal sections taper up and over ıe side windows, sandwiching ıe glass roof. The twin rear ·xhaust pipes are offset to the eft. Engines are 1.6 petrol and ?.0 diesel.

I - SPY points: 20

PORSCHE 911

There has been a Porsche 911 on sale since 1964, and the overall shape of the latest one is a gradual evolution of the simple, classic original. The bonnet dips down between the large oval headlights, and the roof of the car tapers to a gentle finish. The six-cylinder engine is at the back which explains the big slatted air vent on the 911's sloping tail. The 3.8-litre Carrera S can reach almost 190mph. Score for any 911 you see.

 **I - SPY points: 20**

PORSCHE BOXSTER

This Porsche sports car is more affordable than the 911, and is a mid-engined two-seater, which explains the subtle air intakes jus behind the doors. The styling is simple and graceful, and the rea spoiler only reveals itself (it cuts across the rear lights) by rising when the Boxster accelerates pa 75mph. Older Boxsters look fairl similar – score for any you see.

 **I - SPY points: 20**

PORSCHE CAYENNE

This large and impressive 4x4 car has a centre section similar to most other expensive off-roaders, but at the front and the back it has lots in common with Porsche's traditional sports cars, with a sloping bonnet and triangulated headlights level with the bonnet surface. There are petrol and diesel V6 engines and a very powerful petrol V8; you can even order a Cayenne as a petrol-electric hybrid. Despite its height, the Cayenne is a nimble, fast and fine-handling machine.

I - SPY points: 20

PORSCHE PANAMERA

Most luxury saloons are upright and formal-looking, but this big, expensive four-door Porsche is flat and broad. Despite the fact that it looks a bit tail-heavy, with coupe-like side windows and a large flat rear screen, the Panamera has its engine at the front, and both two- and four-wheel drive options are offered. Also unlike other large luxury cars, the Panamera has a hatchback fifth door.

I - SPY points: 40

RANGE ROVER CLASSIC

The very first Range Rover arrived in 1970, and for the next 26 years barely changed at all, which is why this legendary off-roader came to be known as the Classic. It stands tall and has deep windows all round, with the bonnet forming the top part of the wings. In contrast to the severe angular styling, the headlights are always round.

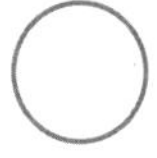
I - SPY points: 15

RANGE ROVER EVOQUE

From its slim cheese-grater grille at the front to its narrow rear screen and 'short' windows the Evoque stands out. The slanted waistline and wide wheelarches make its alloy wheels and tyres look huge. This British-made 4x4 has been a runaway success as the most compact Range Rover ever, and the car is unusual in being available as a two-door coupe and a five-door estate. Try and get a peek at the stylish dashboard.

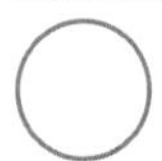
I - SPY points: 20

ANGE ROVER SPORT

his is the sportiest car in the ange Rover line-up. It's slightly maller than the current Range over, and with a considerably ower roofline, but retains the traight-lined styling you would xpect. You'll notice the chrome- urrounded air vents on the front vings, and that the windows nd screen pillars wrap around he car as a dark band. It comes vith V6 diesel or two sizes of V8 etrol engine.

I - SPY points: 15

RENAULT TWIZY

So many things about this city car are unique on British roads today. Obviously, the body is a pod with the wheels jutting out at each corner; there are no doors as standard (they are optional) but hinged side impact bars; and the seating is for two people in tandem. No wonder it is classed by the Government as a 'quadricycle'. And, of course, it is entirely electric, recharged at the mains. Great for the city.

I - SPY points: 35

REVA G-WIZ

The tiny G-Wiz was the first electric car to sell reasonably well in the UK, mainly in London where it is exempt from the Congestion Charge and can park – and sometimes even be recharged – for free. It is a tiny little two-seater that looks like a compressed version of a normal supermini hatchback. Round headlights sit in a one-piece plastic nose section, and the G-Wiz has sliding windows for simplicity and low weight.

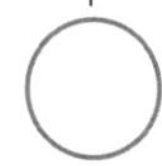

I - SPY points: 25

RENAULT WIND

This exciting little car was only on sale for a 18 months in the UK before being withdrawn, so it's quite a rare spot. The two-seater, which is based on the Twingo, has a one-piece metal roof panel that opens by rotating through 180 degrees before sliding away, to turn the car into an open roadster; the process takes just 12 seconds. The door handles are semi-circular openings, and there is both a roll bar and a rear spoiler behind the cockpit.

I - SPY points: 40

ROLLS-ROYCE PHANTOM

he Phantom is one of the all-
ound biggest cars available –
's a huge, impressive limousine
avoured by millionaires, royalty
nd celebrities. Its front grille
ooks like a model of a Greek
emple, and the famous 'Spirit of
cstasy' flying lady mascot stands
roud above it. Headlights are
ectangles. The rear end of the
ar, in contrast, is graceful and
oft-edged. Look at the wheels
nd see how the Rolls-Royce
mblems stay upright at all times.
his is a truly impressively large
ar when seen on the road.

I - SPY points: 40

SAAB 9-3 CONVERTIBLE

Sadly, Swedish marque Saab no longer manufacture cars, so expect to see fewer and fewer of these characterful cars around in future. However, the 9-3 was always popular in the UK, especially in convertible form like this. The standard 9-3 saloon was a four-door but the convertible has two. The interior has plenty of room for four people as a traditional fabric hood was fitted, which could be stowed away in very little space.

I - SPY points: 15

ŠKODA ROOMSTER

Look at a Škoda Roomster side-on and you'll see this is a compact multi-purpose vehicle (MPV) like no other. The side windows at the back are huge and oddly-shaped, allowing a great view out for the three people in the back. The front windows, meanwhile, are set rather higher. A very simple radiator grille at the front is topped with a chunky chrome strip, with Škoda's emblem set in the middle of it.

 **I - SPY points: 10**

SMART FORTWO

The engine in the Smart is under the two seats, which means the car can be made unusually short, at a little over 2.5m. The contrasting strip that frames the doors gives an indication of the safety cell on to which the Smart body panels are attached. The interiors on early cars (also called the CityCoupe) were futuristic, with dials all in separate pods; recent models have a more conventional dashboard. Many owners find this is the perfect car for city life.

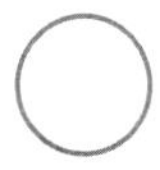 **I - SPY points: 5**

SMART ROADSTER

This very small sports car was on sale between 2003 and 2006, and shared the turbocharged three-cylinder 0.7-litre engine of the Smart city car. The car is very short and low; the Roadster model has a flat panel over the rear engine, the Roadster Coupe has a glazed, boxed-in back end, and both can come with either a removable roof panel or an electrically-operated soft-top. The front lights are set in grey plastic strips set into the bonnet.

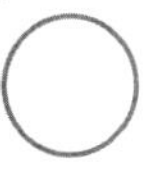

I - SPY points: 20

SUBARU IMPREZA WRX STI

The very latest Subaru Impreza is a five-door hatchback, but the car that got everyone talking about Subaru was a four-door saloon that was made until 2007. In WRX STI form, it was a four-wheel drive, turbocharged 2.0 or 2.5-litre car whose amazing performance had been developed in rallying in the 1990s. You can easily recognise it because it has blistered wheelarches, a big spoiler on the boot lid and a deep front air dam with driving lights set into it. The favoured colour among owners is a rich mid blue.

SUZUKI JIMNY

The cute and upright little Suzuki has been around for years and barely changes. It's a bit like a miniature version of a Land Rover Defender or Jeep Wrangler and, like those two, it has four-wheel drive and stands high off the ground. However, with a small 1.3-litre petrol engine, it's much more economical. The front light clusters make up the square corners of the car, while the rear side window has a distinctive 'chip' off one bottom corner.

I - SPY points: 5

TOYOTA GT86

A compact coupe with tight lines and a long bonnet/short boot look, the GT86 has a neat spoiler at the back and twin exhaust pipes exiting the car through a black diffuser panel below the boot lid. It's designed to be an old-fashioned fun car to drive, which means drive to the rear wheels, no turbocharger on the 2-litre petrol engine and fairly narrow tyres; the cockpit is simple and the rev-counter is the biggest dial...

I - SPY points: 20

TOYOTA IQ

You'll immediately notice that the iQ is very compact. It has three full-size seats and one occasional seat inside. Lots of thought has gone into freeing up space for the cabin, which means it has thinner seats, a compact air-conditioning unit and even a thin, flat fuel tank. The engine is a low-polluting three-cylinder. Almost the whole side of the car is taken up with the large door and, as there is virtually no bonnet or boot, the wheels appear enormous!

I - SPY points: 15

TVR CHIMAERA

On sale until 2005, this beefy two-seater sports car was built in Blackpool, and is the best-selling TVR ever. The styling is curvy, with a line running around the car, below the doors, with sunken 'bites' into it for the grille and indicator lights. See if you can spot the long, thin vents on the edges of the bonnet, there to feed cooling air to the powerful V8 engine underneath, and note there are no door handles; they open using buttons located on the door mirrors.

I - SPY points: 20

VAUXHALL AMPERA

The Ampera is a sister car to the Chevrolet Volt, but has a very different 'face', with boomerang-like sections encasing the headlights and lower driving lights with a black plastic section in between. Just like the Volt, it's a clever 'plug-in hybrid', meaning you can charge it overnight and drive for 50 miles on electric power before you need to switch over to the 1.4-litre petrol engine.

I - SPY points: 30

VAUXHALL MERIVA

This unusual compact MPV (multi-purpose vehicle) has a side window line that is instantly recognisible, as it makes a sudden dip at the back to give a better view out. The Meriva has back doors which are hinged at the rear, so they open outwards like those on the Rolls-Royce Phantom limousine. The rear seats slide backwards and forwards so you can increase boot space.

I - SPY points: 10

VAUXHALL MOKKA

It took Vauxhall quite a while to catch up with its competitors and launch a small 'crossover' but the Mokka finally made it, bearing a name that makes it sound like a coffee bean! Big wheels, a forward-leaning look and chunky lines make it look tough, with a black-painted lower skirt section emphasising the car's height, with an optional four-wheel drive off-road version.

I - SPY points: 30

VAUXHALL VX220

The VX220 has a similar size and shape to the Lotus Elise, which isn't too much of a surprise because both cars share the same bonded aluminium chassis. And they were built side by side in the Lotus factory in Norfolk. The Vauxhall, which comes with or without a turbocharger, looks more solid and boxy than the Lotus, with a simple vertical air intake behind the doors for the mid-mounted engine. It has a bright metal windscreen surround and a lift-out roof panel.

I - SPY points: 30

VOLKSWAGEN BEETLE

The modern Beetle is a common sight all over the UK as both a hatchback and a convertible. So we're making this more of a challenge for you by including the new model here. Newly introduced in 2012 its longer, wider and with a lower roof line than the Beetle it replaces, with more integrated light clusters at the back (the old ones were circular) and a full-width air intake with more angular corners at the front below bumper level. There is a convertible model planned soon.

I - SPY points: 20

VOLKSWAGEN EOS

Volkswagen has made a very neat job of its Eos, which is a Golf-based coupe-convertible with a five-piece folding metal hardtop. It looks just as elegant with the roof up or down, but it is also unique in having a sliding sunroof built in to the metal rooftop panel. Early cars had a small grille at the front but the latest versions have a full-width grille with horizontal slats, quite like the Golf sister car.

I - SPY points: 20

VOLKSWAGEN SCIROCCO

Volkswagen's coupe has its own style, with bodywork appearing to be 'melted' over big alloy wheels, and with narrow side windows giving it a mean and powerful look. Inside, though, it's very spacious and comfortable. The bonnet sits on top of the wings and front air intake like a big, smooth beak. With the most powerful 2.0-litre engine, it's fast too: 149mph top speed and 0-60mph in 6.9sec.

I - SPY points: 15

/OLKSWAGEN TOUAREG

'his large off-roader is named ıfter the nomadic Touareg ›eople of north Africa, which s appropriate as the four-wheel łrive VW is designed to be able ɔ tackle just about any terrain it ›ncounters. The first- and second- ȷeneration cars are quite similar, ınd are notably less aggressive ɔoking than some rivals. The ıew Touareg has unique glare- ree high-beam headlights. ┤aving once towed a Boeing '47 airliner, a Touareg holds ıe record for the heaviest load ›ulled by a passenger car.

I - SPY points: 20

I - SPY points: 20

VOLKSWAGEN UP

Some think VW's new Up is the coolest of all conventional city cars. The quality of this little runabout is outstanding. It's tall and narrow, with body-coloured sections across its radiator grille and across the top of the dashboard, and a contrasting black tailgate that is almost vertical. The 1-litre three-cylinder engine gives it plenty of 'zip' and the front seats are roomy enough for even the tallest people.

VOLVO C70

A folding metal hardtop is the big feature on this full four-seater Swedish convertible from Volvo. Being a very practical car company, though, Volvo has made sure there's also room for plenty of luggage when the roof is folded down by designing in an extra-long boot. The car has a broad 'shoulder line' common to all Volvos and wears its Volvo badge – derived from the ancient symbol for iron – with pride.

I - SPY points: 20

Index

First published by Michelin Maps and Guides 2013
Created and produced by Blue Sky Publishing Limited.

Print services by FingerPrint International Book production – fingerprint@pandora.be
The publisher gratefully acknowledges the contribution of the I-Spy team: Ruth Neilson, Camilla Lovell and Geoff Watts in the production of this title.
The publisher gratefully acknowledges the contribution of Giles Chapman, who compiled the contents, researched the pictures, and wrote the text.
The photographs in this book are sourced from the manufacturers of the vehicles pictured, to whom grateful thanks are acknowledged. Additional photographs were supplied by the Giles Chapman Library. Thanks to Spencer Chapman (aged 10) for his help with what's cool and what's not.
10 9 8 7 6 5 4 3 2 1

HOW TO GET YOUR I-SPY CERTIFICATE AND BADGE

Every time you score 1000 points or more in an I-Spy book, you can apply for a certificate

HERE'S WHAT TO DO, STEP BY STEP:

Certificate

- Ask an adult to check your score
- Ask his or her permission to apply for a certificate
- Apply online to www.ispymichelin.com
- Enter your name and address and the completed title
- We will send you back via e mail your certificate for the title

Badge

- Each I-Spy title has a cut out (page corner) token at the back of the book
- Collect five tokens from different I-Spy titles
- Put Second Class Stamps on two strong envelopes
- Write your own address on one envelope and put a £1 coin inside it (for protection). Fold, but do not seal the envelope, and place it inside the second envelope
- Write the following address on the second envelope, seal it carefully and post to:

I-Spy Books
Michelin Maps and Guides
Hannay House
39 Clarendon Road
Watford
WD17 1JA